The Wonderful World of Poems

Timothy Horne

To order additional copies of this book, contact:
Xlibris
844-714-8691
www.Xlibris.com
Orders@Xlibris.com

ISBN: Softcover   978-1-6698-1181-7
         EBook   978-1-6698-1180-0

Print information available on the last page

Rev. date: 02/11/2022

Contents

The Snowman

3 kids ran out to play in the snow
They were all happy and ready to go
First they made the bottom of the snowman
which they have just began
Next they made the snowman's chest
Then they stopped to take a small rest
Then they put the head on top
And borrowed a hat from dear old pop
Finally, they made the face
They put the coal and carrot in place
Then they said let's call it a day
But will come out later to play
The snowman just stood there happy as could be
Because he had friends like those little 3

The Sand Castle

3 kids ran out to play in the sand

They had their buckets and shovels in hand

First they dug a really deep moat

Then they waved to a passing boat

Next they piled the sand really tall

Then they formed it into a wall

Then they added the 4 corner towers

This part was harder and took several hours

Finally, they made the gate

Then they realized it was getting late

Then they heard their parents say

Come on kids it's the end of the day

When they left the beach there was no one left from the crowd

But their castle was still standing, its red flag flying proud

The Hot Air balloon

3 kids ran out to pick a hot air balloon
They would be flying in one this afternoon
First they picked out their favorite color
They wanted to ride in red more than any other
Next they filled the balloon full of air
watching as it rose high above the fair
then they tied the ropes down tight
Finally, they were ready for their exciting flight
when they got in the basket they saw their dad waving by
As they rose into the sky
On their way back down they heard their dad say
Don't worry you can fly again another day

The Leaf Pile

3 kids ran out to rake the leaves on the ground

They couldn't wait to jump in a giant leaf mound

first they got the rakes from the shed

To rake the leaves orange, yellow and red

Next they picked a spot under the tree

Where they thought the leaf pile should be

Then they raked across the whole lawn

Until every single leaf was gone

finally, the long day of raking was done

So they jumped on in and had hours of fun

At the end of the day their father came out and said

Kids put the rakes back in the shed

when they went inside their leaf pile blew away

But they would rake it again on another autumn day

The Scarecrow

The scarecrow guarded the fields everyday

His job was to scare all the birds away

He would just stand there and stare

and the birds would flee

But there was a world that he wanted to see

He decided I'm not needed here, so he went on the run

He went to see the world's cities and go have some fun

He went to London, Paris and some cities in Spain

And he really enjoyed the ride home on the train

But when he got back what he saw made him sad

All the corn was eaten, the whole harvest gone bad

So when he went back to work the birds were afraid

Because now the scarecrow knew why he was made

The Ice Cream Sundae

The ice cream sundae so yummy and sweet
The ice cream sundae a really nice treat
First you get a menu to read
but please take all the time that you need
When you're ready you have to decide
Chocolate, vanilla or strawberry which one will be tried
Next they scoop the ice cream into your cup
You watch with joy as it starts to fill up
Then you add the fluffy whipped cream
Sprinkles and a cherry to top off your ice cream
The final thing I'd like to know,
is this for here or is this to go
Then add a spoon and your finally done
Enjoy your ice cream everyone

The Seashell

The sad little seashell so plain and so white

He sits on the beach all through the day and the night

All of the other shells have so much color and style

All I have is a spot on this sand pile

All of my friends have been taken away

And so I'm alone at the end of the day

But even now I have hope I'll be found

That some kid will come and pick me up off the ground

Look here comes a kid reaching out for me

I can't believe it, could it really be

He picked me up even though I'm not colored or new

So it just goes to show dreams really can come true

The Explorer

A famous explorer went to a faraway place

To find the treasure of an ancient race

He had to cross a desert of sand

Before he could get to this wondrous land

But once there he found a jungle growing green

It was the greatest sight he'd ever seen

He went in the temple he found at the jungles center

Despite the warning saying not to enter

But once inside he found no gold

Just some writing that was very old

When he read it he would understand

The only treasure was the beauty of the land

And so the explorer decided to stay

And that's where he lives to this very day

The Garbage Truck

The big green garbage truck what does he do

He gets rid of trash for me and for you

All the other cars have jobs that are fun

But the poor garbage truck doesn't feel needed by anyone

The police car gets to chase crooks down the street

And the fire trucks proven it can take on the heat

The ambulance carries people who need urgent care

If you need any of them, you can count on them to be there

But today when he was collecting the trash like before

Something new happened when a man walked out his front door

He came out and thanked him for the fine job he had done

and so it was with every house on the block, every single one

he finally realized it's not about the job that you do

It's about doing your best and always seeing your work through

Ghosts

Ghosts are very rarely seen

Though some have been spotted on Halloween

But what do they look like I bet you will ask

Well a real ghost doesn't hide behind a sheet or a mask

A real ghost is like a white shadow floating around

And if you listen you can hear them make an eerie sound

or sometimes they'll just jump out and yell boo

But don't be scared there just messing with you

But if you really want to meet one face to face

You'll have to find a really spooky place

Because that's where they like to go

What they see in it I'll never know

But don't be afraid most ghosts are fine

Just ask Casper he's a friend of mine

Penny

The poor old penny, all rusted and bent

After a lifetime of being bartered traded and spent

Never in a wallet more than a few days at a time

He just couldn't compete with the nickel, the quarter, and the dime

He'd been used at vending machines, restaurants, and every kind of store

He's even spent some time at the bank locked behind the vault door

after all those years of hardship he'd been broken beyond repair

Now he sits on the sidewalk all alone in despair

It feels like just yesterday he was shiny and new

Being made at the mint in 1972

Then finally one day he was picked up by a kid walking by

with his rust and his dents the penny just couldn't see why

The kid collected coins, so he took him back to his place

There the penny finally felt at home in his shiny new case

The Hot Dog

A hot dog is something we all love to eat

It's always such a wonderful treat

At the carnival you can get one as part of your meal

Just go to the food court next to the big Ferris wheel

At the window you'll see the menu full of goodies you can try

But the hot dog is the one that you're going to buy

First it's cooked on the grill until it's done

Then they put it into the hot dog bun

Next they get all the condiments out

You can add ketchup, mustard and sauerkraut

When your orders ready you can get a side of fries

And a cool refreshing soda of any size

Once you pay the bill you'll be all done

Then you can eat your hot dog and go have some fun

Printed in the United States
by Baker & Taylor Publisher Services